JUN - - 2009

WOODRIDGE PUBLIC LIBRARY

W9-BRO-165

WITHDRAWN

Woodridge Public Library

Caring for Your
Frog

Rennay Craats

Weigl Publishers Inc.

WOODRIDGE PUBLIC LIBRARY
3 PLAZA DRIVE
WOODRIDGE, IL 60517-5014
(630) 964-7899

Project Coordinator
Heather C. Hudak

Design and Layout
Warren Clark
Bryan Pezzi

Copy Editor
Janice L. Redlin

Photo Research
Barbara Hoffman

Locate the frog footprints throughout the book to find useful tips on caring for your pet.

Published by Weigl Publishers Inc.
350 5th Avenue, Suite 3304, PMB 6G
New York, NY 10118-0069 USA
Web site: www.weigl.com

Copyright 2005 WEIGL PUBLISHERS INC.
All rights reserved. No part of this publication may be reproduced, stored in a retrieval system, or transmitted in any form or by any means, electronic, mechanical, photocopying, recording, or otherwise, without the prior written permission of the publisher.

Library of Congress Cataloging-in-Publication Data

Craats, Rennay.
  Caring for your frog / Rennay Craats.
     p. cm. -- (Caring for your pet)
  ISBN 1-59036-218-7 (softcover) 1-59036-198-9 (library bound : alk. paper)
  1. Frogs as pets--Juvenile literature. I. Title. II. Caring for your pet (Mankato, Minn.)
  SF459.F83C73 2004
  639.3'789--dc22

                                   2004001005

                    Printed in the United States of America
                    1 2 3 4 5 6 7 8 9 0   08 07 06 05 04

Photograph and Text Credits
Every reasonable effort has been made to trace ownership and to obtain permission to reprint copyright material. The publishers would be pleased to have any errors or omissions brought to their attention so that they may be corrected in subsequent printings.

Cover: red-eyed tree frog (Tom Stack & Associates/Kitchin & Hurst); **Gerry Bucsis and Barbara Somerville:** page 6R; **Corel Corporation:** pages 10B, 28, 29; ©**Brian Kenney:** page 16; **Dan Nedrelo:** pages 7L, 10T, 11T, 21, 23T; **Photofest (©Warner Bros Inc):** pages 26, 27; **Photos.com:** pages 5T, 5B, 7M, 9B, 14, 15, 17T, 17B, 23B, 24, 25B, 30, 31; **PhotoSpin, Inc.:** pages 13, 22; **Allen Blake Sheldon:** 6L, 6M, 8, 9T, 11B, 12, 18/19, 20, 25T; **Tom Stack & Associates:** pages 1, 3, 7R (Kitchin & Hurst), 4 (Joe McDonald).

All of the Internet URLs given in the book were valid at the time of publication. However, due to the dynamic nature of the Internet, some addresses may have changed, or sites may have ceased to exist since publication. While the author and publisher regret any inconvenience this may cause readers, no responsibility for any such changes can be accepted by either the author or the publisher.

Contents

Frog Fun

Frogs have lived on Earth for millions of years. They come in many shapes and sizes. Each type of frog behaves differently. Some frogs sit very still. They wait for food to come nearby. Others are very active and leap around their environment. In nature, frogs are found in nearly every type of **habitat**. Some frogs climb on rocks. Others swim in the water. Other frogs dig into the ground to create burrows, holes, and tunnels.

Frogs are fragile animals. They cannot be handled often. They prefer to be watched rather than to play with people.

■ Frogs can provide much fun and education for children.

Many people think frogs and toads are the same animals. Actually, all toads are frogs, but not all frogs are toads. Toads live on land. They enter the water only to lay eggs. Frogs make their homes on land as well as in the water. Toads also have no teeth and drier skin than frogs. Toads often have warts all over their bodies.

No matter what kind of frog pet owners choose, these animals provide hours of entertainment. Frogs are popular pets throughout North America. Pet frogs are very different from pet cats or dogs. Frogs do not need to be walked or cuddled. Still, they require love and special care from their owners.

■ Pet frogs can live a long time. Many live between 4 and 15 years.

Fascinating Facts

- Most frogs have unique voices. Male frogs make louder sounds than female frogs.
- Frogs are amphibians. The word *Amphibia* means "dual life." This refers to the two phases of a frog's life. One phase is in the water. The other phase is on land.
- The study of reptiles and amphibians is called herpetology.
- Few frogs have a neck. Only five types of African frogs have necks.

Pet Profiles

Frogs live in most areas of the world. The only places frogs do not thrive are **Antarctica**, very dry deserts, and some oceanic islands. There are more than 4,500 different frog and toad species in the world. Not all of these species make good pets. People can create great homes for many types of frogs and keep their pets happy.

GREEN AND BLACK DART-POISON FROG

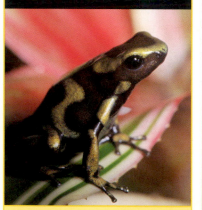

- Grows up to 2.5 inches (6.35 centimeters) long
- Green with black bands or blotches
- Lives in Costa Rica, Panama, and Colombia
- Some are poisonous to humans
- Other dart-poison frog types include the blue, red and black, strawberry, and dyeing dart-poison frogs

RED-EYED TREE FROG

- Grows to about 3 inches (7.62 cm) long
- Lime green body, greenish-blue legs with red or orange feet, and cream and blue stripes on its stomach
- Bright red eyes
- Most live between central Mexico and northern Honduras, as well as from the Caribbean to Panama

WHITE DUMPY TREE FROG

- Grows to about 4 inches (10 cm) long
- Has bright green skin
- Lives in northeastern Australia, Indonesia, and New Guinea
- **Nocturnal**
- Makes a good pet for first-time frog owners

Each year, scientists discover about twelve new frog species. Scientists may continue to discover new species for many more years. As long as frog habitats are protected from human development, new frog species will likely be discovered.

Many frogs live in warm and tropical climates. In the San Cecilia basin in Ecuador, scientists found 81 frog and toad species. This is about the same number of frog species found in the entire United States.

SPRING PEEPERS

- Grows to about 1.5 inches (3.81 cm) long
- Brown, tan, or gray with a dark, X-shaped marking on its back and a white, cream, or yellow belly
- Lives in ponds, marshes, and woodlands throughout the Great Lakes region
- Changes color according to its mood or surroundings

TOMATO FROG

- Grows up to 4 inches (10.16 cm) long
- Reddish-orange with bright red or black markings on its throat
- Nocturnal
- One of the most popular pet frog species
- Lives in Madagascar

AMERICAN BULLFROG

- Largest North American frog species, growing up to 7 inches (17.78 cm) long
- Dull green or brown skin
- Sounds like a bull
- Lives east of the Rockies and has spread to the Pacific coast; introduced in Italy, Europe, Cuba, West Indies, and Hawaii
- Lives in the water and on land

Former Frogs

Among the fierce tyrannosaurus rex and the tame brachiosaurus hopped a familiar creature. Frog **ancestors** made their mark on Earth more than 400 million years ago. They lived during the time of the dinosaurs. Frogs survived even after the dinosaurs became **extinct**. Scientists have found **fossils** that suggest that modern-day frogs have been on Earth for between 208 million and 144 million years. Frogs developed from early amphibians. Amphibians are animals that are able to live both in water and on land. Amphibians have not changed much over time. Scientists believe that ancient frogs grew jumping legs to avoid being eaten by dinosaurs.

The bright colors on some frogs act as a warning to **predators**. These colorful species are often poisonous.

■ Cranwell's horned frog is also called the Pac-Man frog.

Like all amphibians, frogs are **cold-blooded** animals. They are four-legged, air-breathing, tailless creatures. They are also vertebrates. This means they have a backbone. These fascinating animals are the most studied amphibians. In many areas, frogs live in backyard gardens and ponds. People can buy frogs at pet stores. For decades, frogs have been fun and popular pets.

■ Red-eyed tree frogs are also known as "monkey frogs" because they have good coordination.

Fascinating Facts

- The largest frog is the West African Goliath frog. It measures nearly 12 inches (30.48 cm) long and weighs more than 6.5 pounds (2.95 kilograms). The smallest frog is the gold frog, which measures only 0.38 inch (1 cm).
- There are more than 40 families of frogs and toads. Only some of these frogs and toads make good pets.
- Most frogs are harmless to people. Some create deadly **secretions**. These secretions protect frogs from attack by other animals or humans. Some frog toxins are among the most poisonous substances on Earth.

Life Cycle

Young frogs are called tadpoles. Tadpoles and frogs do not look alike. In fact, if you saw a tadpole and a frog together, you might not know they are the same animal. As frogs mature, they pass through a process called **metamorphosis**. They begin their lives as eggs. Then they enter a fish-like state. Finally, they develop into frogs.

Eggs

In the spring, female frogs respond to the mating call of male frogs. The male and female frogs mate in the water. The female produces eggs. The male **fertilizes** the eggs, which float in strings or bunches. These strings or bunches may attach to plants or rocks in the water. Many frog species lay thousands of eggs at one time. The eggs immediately begin developing into tadpoles.

Adult Frogs

At 16 weeks of age, metamorphosis is complete. This means the froglets are adult frogs. Frogs live on land, but most species spend a great deal of time in or near the water. Many frogs are fully grown by 3 or 4 years of age. About 1 year after metamorphosis is complete, frogs often return to the water to mate and lay eggs.

Fascinating Facts

- Many frog species lay eggs in wet places on land.
- Some frogs, such as the leopard frog, lay 4,000 eggs at one time. This increases the chance of an egg reaching the frog stage.
- Some frogs can live 15 to 20 years in captivity. Other frogs live only a few years.

Tadpoles

Eggs hatch between 6 and 21 days after fertilization. When they first hatch, tadpoles do not have a specific shape. As they grow, tadpoles develop flat tails and round mouths. Tadpoles live in the water. They breathe through gills. Tadpoles begin swimming and eating algae, or seaweed, 7 to 10 days after they hatch. Four weeks after the tadpoles hatch, skin begins to cover their gills. When the tadpoles are 6 to 9 weeks of age, they begin growing legs and arms. The tadpoles now look like small frogs with long tails.

Froglets

When tadpoles are 12 weeks old, they are called froglets. Froglets' tails have almost disappeared. Froglets look like small adult frogs. They are preparing to leave the water to begin their lives on land.

Picking Your Pet

Picking the perfect pet frog is a big decision. There are many factors to consider when choosing a frog. A pet frog, if well cared for, will be part of the family for many years. Researching these leaping buddies will help answer questions about what to look for when buying a frog.

What Will a Frog Cost?

Some pet stores may not carry a wide variety of frog species. Specialty stores or breeders sell many kinds of common and rare frog species. The cost of a pet frog depends on the species. Rare species are more expensive to purchase.

There are many other costs to consider when purchasing a pet frog. The frog's house is the largest expense. The enclosure and its accessories can cost hundreds of dollars. Once these items are purchased, it is not expensive to keep a frog. Frogs do not cost much to buy. Small frogs eat insects, while large species may eat other small animals. Unlike other pets, such as cats and dogs, frogs do not require regular visits to a **veterinarian**. This helps keep costs down, too.

Always ask to see a frog eat before buying it. If the frog does not eat or has trouble eating, it may be a sign of a serious health problem.

■ Blue dart-poison frogs were once very rare. They are now easier to find and cheaper to buy.

Learning about frogs before bringing one home will help you meet all of your pet's needs.

Do I Have Time for a Frog?

Frogs do not need much attention from their owners. Still, owners need to set time aside each day to give their pet basic care. Owners need to make sure their frog has fresh food and water. This requires frequent trips to the pet store to buy live food. Owners also need to check the temperature and humidity, or moisture, inside the enclosure. Owners need to clean their frog's enclosure, too.

How Do I Choose the Right Frog for Me?

It is a good idea for first-time frog owners to purchase a more common frog species. These species are easier to care for and they live happily in captivity. After 1 or 2 years, owners can buy rare frog species. Owners should also consider the frog's diet when choosing a pet. Some frogs eat live mice or other small animals. Owners have to be comfortable handling these animals, too.

Fascinating Facts

- Frogs and toads can be purchased at pet stores, through breeders and importers, and at trade shows. Pet owners should do research to make sure they are buying from reputable dealers.
- In the United States, American bullfrogs, leopard frogs, and green frogs are great starter pets.
- When replacing water in the enclosure, allow it to sit for 1 day before allowing the frog near the water. This ensures there is no chlorine in the water.
- When choosing a frog, owners should look for frogs that eat well, have open, alert eyes, have normal coloring and skin texture, will hop, and appear plump and healthy.

Amphibian Abode

Some frogs live entirely in the water. An ordinary aquarium makes a good enclosure for these frogs. **Aquatic** frogs swim around underwater and then float on the surface to breathe.

Some frogs live in water and on land. They require shallow water pools inside their enclosures. They also need rocks for climbing. Create a smooth rock or gravel slope on one side of the enclosure. Place a plastic bowl of water on the other side of the enclosure. This creates a beach for frogs that enjoy spending some time in the water as well as on land. Frogs that live mostly on land need only small water bowls. Branches, hearty plants, or driftwood are great additions inside the enclosure. Frogs can climb on these objects.

Always use gravel or pebbles with smooth edges in your frog's enclosure. Frogs can scratch or cut themselves on sharp edges. This can lead to serious infections.

■ If you plan to keep more than one frog in an aquarium, they should be the same species.

Land frogs' enclosures are called terrariums. Terrariums are glass tanks with screen lids. Digging frogs need very clean soil inside their enclosures. The soil must be deep enough for the frogs to bury themselves. Discard the soil when you clean the frog's enclosure. Place fresh soil inside the enclosure.

There are many other items that can be placed inside a frog enclosure. Frogs enjoy rain, so it is a good idea to place a misting machine over the enclosure. Owners can spray water over their frogs each day, too. A **filtration system** helps keep the water clean. Owners need to make sure the temperature in the aquarium is comfortable and safe for the frog. Thermometers monitor the terrarium's temperature. Frogs prefer moderate temperatures. If owners live in a cold climate, they can use a heating pad or heating lamps to raise the temperature inside the enclosure.

Frogs are shy creatures, so it is important to make sure your pet has a hiding place.

Fascinating Facts

- It is a good idea to cover your pet's enclosure with a screen. This keeps fresh air circulating. It also prevents heat and humidity from building up inside the enclosure.
- Frogs do not need to drink from water dishes. They breathe and drink through their skin.
- Some frogs can drown. Water features should not be too deep. The frog should be able to sit with its head above the water.
- A 10-gallon (37.85-liter) tank can house five 1-inch (2.54-cm) long frogs or one 5-inch (12.7-cm) long frog.

Frog Fare

Frogs are easy to please when it comes to mealtime. Many frogs are insectivores. This means they eat insects. They prefer to eat live insects. Crickets, grasshoppers, fruit flies, and moths are great frog food. Frogs also eat spiders and earthworms. Some frog owners raise their own feeder insects or collect them from outdoors. These bugs must be carefully selected. Owners should make sure insects have not been treated with fertilizers, pesticides, herbicides, or other harmful substances.

Many frogs need a large amount of food each day. Live feeder insects may be more difficult to find in colder climates or seasons.

▬ Frogs need fresh food and water daily.

Large frog species eat larger animals. Some frogs eat mice, birds, and snakes. Frogs will often try to eat any food item they are given. If they do not like the food, they spit it out. This helps owners know what foods their frog prefers.

Frogs do not have chewing teeth. They have only small cone teeth along their top jaws. There are no teeth on their bottom jaws. This makes chewing impossible. Instead, frogs swallow their meals whole. They use their eyeballs to force food down. Frogs close their bulging eyes and pull them inside their head. Their eyeballs apply pressure to the food, which pushes the food down the frog's throat.

■ Frogs eat a variety of insects, including moths and grasshoppers.

Fascinating Facts

- Horned frogs will eat nearly any item they can fit inside their mouths.
- Tadpoles can be meat-eaters, plant-eaters, or both, depending on the species.
- Many frog species will not eat dead animals. Wiggling a dead animal in front of a frog may fool the frog into thinking the animal is alive.
- Keeping different types of frogs in one enclosure may cause problems. Large frogs sometimes eat smaller frogs.
- A frog uses his sticky tongue to catch insects. The frog flicks his tongue out at the insect. Once the insect becomes stuck to the frog's tongue, the frog pulls the meal into his mouth.

Frog Features

Frog species look different from one another. Some frogs are small and thin. Others are large and broad. Although they have different appearances and behaviors, they share many common features.

A frog absorbs water and oxygen through her skin. **Mucus** glands help keep the frog's skin moist. Poison glands in her skin help protect the frog from enemies. These poisons are toxic to predators, but they do not often affect humans. A frog's skin is very sensitive to heat and cold, too.

Frogs move by jumping. Frogs' legs are strong and powerful. Many frog species can jump very long distances. Frogs have four fingers on their front limbs and five on their back limbs. Frogs that live in water often have webbing between their toes. Most frogs are great swimmers. They use their back legs to push themselves through the water. Their front limbs stay at their sides while they swim.

NORTHERN LEOPARD FROG

Frogs have a scent organ, called the Jacobson's organ, on the roof of their mouth. They use this organ to identify prey. This sense organ tells the frog when food is near by. The Jacobson's organ also detects the odors that predators produce.

Frogs' pupils can be round, vertical, horizontal, or heart-shaped. Their eyes blend in with their skin. This makes it more difficult for predators to find and attack the frogs' eyes. Frogs' eyes are in sockets on the tops and sides of their heads. They can see left, right, and partly behind their head. Frogs can see 50 feet (15.24 m) into the distance, but they cannot see nearby objects. Frogs have movable eyelids and a membrane, or thin layer of tissue, that covers their eyes. This protects their eyes when they are under water. Frogs can partially see through this membrane.

Frog Frets

Frogs are not cuddly pets. They should not be held often. Frogs have sensitive skin, and the oils in human hands can harm their skin. Many frog species may also bite. There are times when handling a pet frog is necessary. For example, owners need to remove their frog from her enclosure in order to clean the enclosure. Owners should be careful when picking up and moving frogs. Since oils from human hands can harm a frog's skin, owners should wear non-powdered, disposable gloves when handling their frog.

Fish nets work well to scoop frogs out of their enclosures. Use one net to catch the frog. Place another net over top of the opening to prevent the frog from jumping out of the net. Then, place the frog in a plastic bowl until the enclosure is clean. Place a screen over the bowl so the frog does not hop away.

Always wash your hands with hot, soapy water, and rinse them well before and after handling your pet frog. This will help keep you and your pet safe from **bacteria**.

When handling a frog, be careful not to let her jump from your hands. This may cause injury to the frog.

Large frog species are easier to handle. Owners can hold these species around the frog's waist. This allows the frog to keep her back legs straight. Many types of frogs will wiggle around and try to escape from their owner's hands. Owners should be careful not to hold their frog too tightly.

Very small frog species, such as dart-poison frogs, should not be held or picked up. They are too fragile. Handling these frogs can injure them. To remove these frogs from their enclosures, use a straw or the soft eraser tip of a pencil to guide the frog into a plastic tube. Place a cork over the open end of the tube. Be sure to poke holes in one end of the tube so the frog can breathe. This is a safe way to move small frogs into their temporary homes.

Some frogs are hard to handle because they are small in size or have slippery skin.

Fascinating Facts

- Pet frogs should never be released into nature. If the natural environment houses different frog species, the newly released frog may cause harm to these species. Frogs living in the natural area can also cause harm to pet frogs.
- Making sure there is water and a moderate temperature inside a frog's enclosure is very important. Frogs can die if it is too hot inside their enclosure or if there is too little water. Frogs need to keep their skin moist.
- Some frogs do not mind being held. Tree frogs will stand on a person's arm or hand. It makes them feel like they are home—up in the air on a tree branch.
- Some frogs bite when handled. These bites are not very painful, but they can startle the person. Startled people often react by jumping or shaking their hand. This can cause injury to the frog if he falls.

Healthy and Happy

Frogs do not need much care. They do not need to be groomed, walked, or visit a veterinarian regularly. Still, owning a pet frog is a big responsibility. Feeding a pet frog the proper amount of the correct food helps keep the frog fit. Making sure the frog's enclosure is clean also helps keep the frog happy and healthy. Owners must clean their pet's enclosure and decorations each month. Frogs release toxins that can build up inside the enclosure. Regular cleaning removes toxins and bacteria that can make the frog ill.

Running tap water for a few minutes before collecting it for the enclosure can lessen the presence of metals, such as zinc, copper, or lead. These metals can poison frogs.

All frogs secrete toxins. Most toxins are not harmful to humans. Some may be deadly or cause mild rashes.

Even if they are properly cared for, frogs can still become ill. Pet frogs can get many bacterial and **fungal** diseases and infections. Some illnesses can be treated with creams or changes to the frog's diet. Owners should contact a veterinarian if they notice changes in their frog's appearance or behavior.

Scientists believe many frog species are being threatened by environmental changes caused by humans.

Veterinarians can treat cuts or find out why a frog may not be eating. They can also give advice about ways to make sure pet frogs are healthy and happy in their captive environment. Frog owners should try to find a veterinarian who specializes in reptiles and amphibians.

Fascinating Facts

- Pet frogs can suffer from a blocked **intestine**. Sometimes, gravel or sand gets mixed into a frog's food. This causes a blockage. Eating too many hard-shelled insects can also cause this problem.
- Frog and toad populations are decreasing in nature. Scientists are studying the reasons for this decline.
- Frogs are sensitive creatures. Owners should use only hot water and colorless paper towels to clean their pet's enclosure.
- Janidan fur frogs look like large, fur-covered frogs. Like mammals, these frogs are warm-blooded animals.

Frog Behavior

Just like people, frogs have different personalities. Some frogs are very active. Others prefer to sit quietly. Some frogs eat a large amount of food every day, while others eat every few days. Still, different frog species share many of the same **traits**.

Some frogs **hibernate** or **estivate**. Some species hibernate when the temperature is very cold. Others estivate when the temperature is very hot. Frogs bury themselves in the ground and will not come out. They do not eat or swim. Their heart rate slows down and they stop moving. Frogs hibernate and estivate to save energy until the temperature is more comfortable. Frogs can remain in this state for a few days or weeks.

If a pet frog buries himself in the ground, you should not be concerned. Do not try to dig him out or force him to eat. Just make sure there is fresh water and food ready when the frog comes out on his own.

Pet Peeves

Frogs do not like:
- being handled often
- having bright lights on all day and night
- having dirty water in their enclosures

Many frogs are active at night when the temperature is cooler and there is more moisture in the air than during the day.

Another shared frog behavior is **molting**. Frogs shed their skin. Some shed their skin every day. They begin by eating the skin around their mouths. Then they eat the rest of their skin. Other frogs pull off pieces of skin from their bodies. Shedding skin is natural and so is eating the skin. Any skin the frog does not eat should be removed from the enclosure.

When molting, some frogs yawn, swell up, and drag their arms up over their head.

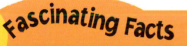

Fascinating Facts

- Frogs are fantastic jumpers. They can leap more than twenty times their own length. This is the same as a 5-foot (1.52-meters) tall person jumping 100 feet (30.48 m).
- Some tree frogs have sticky disks on their fingers and toes. This helps them grip surfaces when they climb.
- Some frog species produce a great deal of **glycerol**. Glycerol acts as a form of antifreeze for the frog's cells. It keeps the frog from freezing in cold temperatures. Frogs that produce glycerol have been frozen in blocks of ice for months. They recovered after being thawed.

Froggy Tales

People have written fairy tales about frogs for centuries. In China, parents tell their children about a frog that was born to human parents. The frog became an emperor. The Frog Prince is a North American and European fairy tale about a prince who is trapped inside a frog's body. Only a kiss from a maiden can reverse the spell that turned the handsome prince into a frog.

Many ancient cultures believed frogs controlled the weather. Some cultures believed that frogs brought rain. Others thought frogs represented thunder in animal form. In Japan, people believed frogs brought good luck.

Fascinating Facts

- *The Tale of Mr. Jeremy Fisher* by Beatrix Potter tells about the adventures of a frog named Mr. Jeremy Fisher. Jeremy Fisher is nearly eaten by two fish while fishing on a pond one day. He returns home empty handed, and has dinner with friends.

■ Michigan J. Frog has been the official mascot of the WB television network since the 1990s.

Not all myths and stories about frogs are happy. Some cultures believed frogs and toads were evil. Other cultures believed frogs could predict the mood of the upcoming year. For example, if the first frog a person sees in spring is on dry ground, he or she will have a sad year. If the frog jumps toward the person, he or she will have many friends.

Frogs have appeared in books, movies, and television series. Kermit the Frog is the most famous frog in the world. Kermit made his first television appearance in a special titled *Hey Cinderella* in 1969. Kermit is the star of *The Muppet Show* and *The Muppet Movie*. He also appears on *Sesame Street*.

■ In 1979's *The Muppet Movie*, Kermit the Frog and his friend Fozzie Bear travel across the United States to Hollywood.

His Royal Frogness

The Frog Prince is a fairy tale about a princess who loses her ball in a spring. A frog living in the spring offers to retrieve the ball if the princess promises to care for him. She agrees but forgets once he returns her ball. The frog follows the girl home—knocking on the door and asking to enter. The king tells his daughter she must keep her word and allow the frog to live in the castle. The frog eats from the princess's plate and sleeps upon her pillow for 3 nights. On the fourth morning, the frog is gone and in his place sleeps a young prince. The prince tells the princess a spell was cast upon him, turning him into a frog until a princess allowed him to stay with her for 3 days. The prince and princess live happily ever after.

From the Brothers Grimm's *The Frog Prince*.

Pet Puzzlers

What do you know about frogs? If you can answer the following questions correctly, you may be ready to own a frog.

Q How many types of frogs and toads live in the world?

There are about 4,500 different types of frogs and toads. New species are discovered every year.

Q What are the major differences between tadpoles and adult frogs?

Tadpoles breathe through gills, live in the water, eat only plants, and have a tail.

Q In which areas do frogs not live?

Frogs do not live in Antarctica, very dry deserts, and some oceanic islands.

Q Why is it important to keep a frog's skin wet?

Frogs breathe and drink through their skin. Moist skin protects the frog.

Q Why is it better not to handle a pet frog often?

Oils from your hands can harm a frog's sensitive skin. Holding them too tightly can injure frogs. Holding them too loose can allow frogs to jump out of your hands and become hurt. Some frogs bite when they are held, too.

Q What do frogs eat?

Some frogs eat insects, such as crickets, grasshoppers, and flies. Others eat birds, mice, snakes, and even other frogs.

Flashy Frogs

Before you buy your pet frog, write down some frog names you like. Some names may work better for a female frog. Others may suit a male frog. Here are just a few suggestions:

Kermit
Prince
Frogger
Charlie
Madeline
Ribbit
Neon
Lily
Legs
Hopper

Frequently Asked Questions

What can I do if my frog will not eat?

If your frog is not eating, it may be a sign that she is ill. When the frog is feeling well, her appetite often returns. To prevent your frog from becoming ill, keep her enclosure clean of bacteria. You can try encouraging your frog to eat by handfeeding her. Wiggle food in front of your frog to see if the frog will eat it. If this does not work, talk to a veterinarian about the problem.

Can I play outside with my frog?

If your frog is a species that lives in your area naturally, you can take your frog outside. If your frog naturally lives in a different environment, do not take her outside. It may cause harm to other frog species living in the area.

Can I house different frog species in the same enclosure?

Some frog species live well together. Others do not. Some frogs have toxins in their skin. These toxins are dangerous or deadly to other frog species. Research different species to make sure they live well together.

More Information

Animal Organizations

You can help frogs stay healthy and happy by learning more about them. Many organizations are dedicated to teaching people how to care for and protect their pet pals. For more frog information, write to the following organizations:

A Thousand Friends of Frogs
Center for Global Environmental Education
Hamline University Graduate School
of Education
1536 Hewitt Avenue
St. Paul, MN 55104-1284

Association for Reptilian and
Amphibian Veterinarians
PO Box 605
Chester Heights, PA 19017

Web Sites

To answer more frog questions, go online and surf to the following Web sites:

All About Frogs for Kids and Teachers
www.kiddyhouse.com/themes/frogs

Frogland
http://allaboutfrogs.org/weird/general/cycle.html

Frogs
www.exploratorium.edu/frogs

Words to Know

ancestors: animals from the past that are related to modern animals

Antarctica: the continent that surrounds the South Pole

aquatic: living in or near water

bacteria: one-celled organisms that can only be seen through a microscope

cold-blooded: having a body temperature that changes with the surroundings

estivate: a sleep-like state entered in extremely hot temperatures

extinct: no longer existing anywhere on Earth

fertilizes: makes able to produce

filtration system: a device used to remove dirt by passing through a porous material

fossils: the rocklike remains of ancient animals and plants

fungal: a plant-like organism that appears as fuzz on the skin

glycerol: a liquid used to preserve something; antifreeze

habitat: natural environment of an animal or plant

hibernate: to enter a sleep-like state that can last through the winter

intestine: long tube-shaped section of the stomach

metamorphosis: a change in form

molting: making room for new growth by shedding hair, feathers, or skin

mucus: a slimy substance

nocturnal: active at night

predators: animals that hunt other animals for food

secretions: substances that are created and released by the body

traits: distinct features

veterinarian: animal doctor

Index

3 1524 00521 9458